TEN THOUSAND THINGS

TEN THOUSAND THINGS
EMILY CRITCHLEY

BOILER HOUSE PRESS

To daughters

Concerning Earth, the mother of all, shall I sing, firm Earth, eldest of Gods, that nourishes all things in the world; all things that fare on the sacred land, all things in the sea, all flying things, all are fed out of her store. Through thee, revered Goddess, are men happy in their children and fortunate in their harvest. Thine it is to give or to take life from mortal men. Happy is he whom thou honourest with favouring heart; to him all good things are present innumerable: his fertile field is laden, his meadows are rich in cattle, his house filled with all good things. Such men rule righteously in cities of fair women...

— From 'To Earth, the Mother of All', *The Homeric Hymns*, trans. Andrew Lang (1899)

THE ORIGIN OF THE <u>WOMAN</u> OF ART
after Martin Heidegger

If, however, the reality of the <u>woman</u> is determined by nothing other than what is at work in the <u>woman</u>, how do things stand with regard to our project of searching out the real <u>woman</u> in <u>her</u> reality? As long as we supposed the reality of the <u>woman</u> to lie primarily in <u>her</u> thingly substructure, we went astray.

First, the prevailing concepts of the thing represent an inadequate means of grasping the thingly element in the <u>woman</u>.

Second, the thingly substructure, which we wanted to treat as the most evident reality of the <u>woman</u> does not, in that way, belong to the <u>woman</u> at all.

As soon as we become fixated on finding such an element in the <u>woman</u> we have unwittingly taken the <u>woman</u> as equipment to which we then ascribe a superstructure supposed to contain what is artistic about <u>her</u>. But the <u>woman</u> is not a piece of equipment that is fitted out in addition with aesthetic worth adhering to <u>her</u>. The <u>woman</u> is no more that than the mere thing is a piece of equipment minus the marks of authentic equipmentality – usefulness and being made.

Our posing the question of the <u>woman</u> has been disturbed by the fact that we asked, not about the <u>woman</u> but, rather, half about a thing and half about equipment. That, however, was not a way of raising the question first developed by us. This way of raising the question belongs, rather to aesthetics. The way in which aesthetics is disposed, in advance, to view the <u>woman</u> stands within the dominion of the traditional interpretation of beings in general. But to disturb this familiar mode of questioning is not what is essential. What really matters is that we open our eyes to the fact that the <u>woman</u>liness of the <u>woman</u>, the equipmentality of equipment, and the thingliness of the thing come nearer to us only when we think the being of beings. A condition of this is that the limits imposed by self-evidence first fall away and that current pseudo-concepts be set aside. This is why we had to take a roundabout route. But it brings us directly onto the path that may lead to a determination of the thingly aspect of the <u>woman</u>. The thingly in the <u>woman</u> should not be denied out of existence; rather, given that it belongs already to the <u>woman</u>-being of the <u>woman</u>, it must be thought out of that <u>woman</u>-being. If this is so, then the path to the determination of the thingly reality of the <u>woman</u> runs not from thing to <u>woman</u> but from <u>woman</u> to thing.

The <u>woman</u> opens up, in <u>her</u> own way, the being of beings. This opening up, i.e., unconcealing, i.e., the truth of beings, happens in the <u>woman</u>. In the <u>woman</u>, the truth of beings has set itself to the <u>woman</u>. <u>Woman</u> is the setting-<u>her</u>self-to-work of truth. What is truth itself, that it happens, at times, as <u>woman</u>? What is this setting-<u>her</u>self-to-work?

Is the <u>woman</u> in <u>her</u>self ever accessible? In order for this to happen it would be necessary to remove the <u>woman</u> from all relation to anything other than <u>her</u>self in order to let <u>her</u> stand on <u>her</u> own and for <u>her</u>self alone. But that is already the innermost intention of the artist. Through <u>her</u>, the <u>woman</u> is to be released into <u>her</u> purest standing-in-<u>her</u>self. Precisely in great <u>women</u> (which is all we are concerned with here) the artist remains something inconsequential in comparison with the <u>woman</u> – almost like a passageway which, in the creative process, destroys itself for the sake of the coming forth of the <u>woman</u>.

AFTERTHOUGHTS

HELLO POEM

Hello poem
You are expensive

Hello poem
I cannot remember

Hello poem
Compartmentalizing the silence

Hello poem
To be a mama means breaking off –

Hello poem
I no longer fit inside you

Hello poem
You no longer fit inside me

Hello poem
I miss you!

Hello poem
Do you miss me?

Hello poem
My old friend

Hello poem
The other night I found myself alone. You weren't near

Hello poem
You kicked me in the head till I woke

Hello poem
You're such a needy baby

Hello poem
We play at silence games. You win

Hello poem
My silhouette makes you out / chases you down the hill

Hello poem
Suddenly traffic

Hello poem
Togetherness pillow

Hello poem
Glue echolocation

Hello poem
You exist! You will!

Hello poem
Hello poem
Hello poem

RETURN TO POETRY
for Marianne Morris

I return here after years spent shouting in the *agora*
til my voice grew hoarse
from where I woke without words or illusions.

The dream of equality is much too big for a poem to take
any such narratives aren't real
as the search for the breadknife or wondering which bills to
    hide or baby
jumping at my sides.

And laws that are laid down as they are exactly
and because you can see everything that's wrong with them,
    but also each of the alternatives.
Inside this room
the difference between speech and act won't signify.

Arguing so long about the trees, they forgot the wood,
its leaves and blue shimmer; how it was not just a resource
    for our having
but a place of variousness, beauty and life.

I wash the dust from my hands and knees,
the sweat from my eyes,
lie down to peel a potato with my head still spinning –
choose a dress from out the periodic table;
forget about poetry.

SOMETHING WONDERFUL HAS HAPPENED
IT IS CALLED YOU

And mostly these days I just like to look
at you and sometimes make words
out of your name or rock you
in my arms till the thought of I
with or without poetry
no longer matters.
It's not like I have forgotten
how to worry

  – the disappearing forests
    vanishing species
    zone of sky above our heads –

I pray that when you are older there may still be
the forests, for instance, and the species

  – precious zone of sky
    to keep sun off yr precious face –

And not just in the zoo.
I worry about other things too but mostly
it is hard to be unhappy these days
especially now the spring's advancing
and you're learning
about hands, how to hold things in them
and take everything it's yours.

UNTITLED (FEAR POEM)

In the exact instance of hollow
exactly another
feels less though alive / more needs
    yet cannot be helped
some voluntary wilderness /

Dear baby, hello.

Audacity of shape
in cold breeding
this, way + half as much again
    but for the first time
curves of a test site /
stratigraphically speaking /

Dear baby, hello.

Clammy reasonable will
suspended
    a curve ball
    a real dusie
struck
then down at the earth,
head for the time
being, no, feeling /

Dear baby, hello.

AFTER ANN LAUTERBACH

The days are creative
The days are successful

I put my lot to bed
with a sigh

I tuck it in:
another successful day!
to add to the little pile

The days are successful
The pile is mounting

The washing's in the freezer
The dinner's in a book

The days are creative
The days are successful

The piano eyes me
from its corner –
colluding with the past
/ all those other plans

The days are creative
The days are successful

Paints are dusty
in the hall cupboard
Poems march around unborn

The days are successful
The pile is mounting

My daughter's new spirit
has designs of its own
– nothing to do with me
– no excuse to hide behind

The days are creative
The days are successful

In haste I iron the floor
In haste (with tears) drop birdseed in the crockery
How many little lives depend on me!
What a successful day!

The hours are long
The hours are long
They whip round before you're almost looking.

UNTITLED (LOVE POEM)
for Peter Hughes

You are there without judgment, poem, for all the coming and going
all the whenevers
all the beauty or the ugly
the rage or the happy
the world, this phantasmagoria.

If it is true illusion in the most sacred sense of the word
what is your part of all this
blame? Why you so private yet
of it
but are you not?

No one will listen to you now.
You cannot be corrupted, monopolized or merged,
you cannot even be held
(you crush the hands that bear you up).
Nor will you fit
into a split second. Consumerized.

You are like those children growing under a great tree
centuries from now. Just wait.

THAT MEANS YOU WORLD (PART I)
for Alec Finlay

Between the indifference of world
& its cruelty

                              connecting us to everything
                              connecting us to nothing

Between the rotation of the sun
& its radiation

                    & I desire that no misery might befall my daughter

(O but world)

                              we must stop thinking ourselves

(invulnerable)

                              we must stop ourselves unthinking

Between deserted futures
& the flood

                              into a cloud
                              a burst

                    a nothing
                    into

And our present
action
is
a whole history of peoples

            even if you have children
            though you have your children's children
            even you yourselves

(why is this self-slaughter
coming from)

In a moment
little

            less than a minute's clock slice!

Quite predictable
very human
of this world yet not of it

            not thinking
            changing
            not changing
            undoing

    As if it were not good!

AFTERTHOUGHT

There is now this film
over everything rainbow
of gilt it brightens
the simple objects
gulf of hope also
it's slippery has its
way with or with
out you lets spill or
let slip or split
up like retracts
it does not
glows bright it will not
is flimsy a puddle is not
is nothing if not
everything can not
eats up the fisheries
sticks to sand particles
claws at poor birds' lungs
and will not ignore yet
we ignore do not
can't ignore should not
won't ignore if not
there'll be no more trust under water.

Not missing but seeing
for the trees the trees the trees the trees the trees
the tree trunks tree branches tree buds the trees
tree leaves the trees the trees tree houses tree stumps tree money
the trees the roots the trees the trees
tree tops tree wood wood forest
the wood the wood the wood
the wood the wood the wood
would miss but would not
would hope but could not
not missing but seeing
not missing but thinking
not missing but being
before the cut cut off
before the cut cut off
the cut the cut the cut
the cut the cut making
the cut
the cut
the cut
/ & deeper into the forest

But in that space were there birds (mangrove cuckoo, white-tailed
    nightjar, ruby humming)
& in that tree were there bats (fruit-eating, yellow-shouldered,
    little big-eyed)
& in that tree were there snakes (rainbow boa, checkerbelly)
the lowland paca / brazilian porcupine
the red-tailed squirrel / common opossum
the southern tamandua / silky anteater
the armidillo / tufted capuchin
whole ordinary species

whole community branches
intercapillary branches
interlocking necessities
still to be found on both these islands
still extant on both these islands
/ before it was broken broken broken broken broken
& it was broken broken broken broken broken

So we came into the forest not seeing but selling
we came into that forest not believing but breaking
not seeing but breaking not breaking but cutting
       / & deeper into the forest

      & again in the forest
      & further into the forest
      & the birds move along
      the bats move along
      snakes move along
      peoples move along
   along along again along along
   along again along along along
   / til they come to the end of forest

      But what happens at the end
   of intercapillary branches are breaking
   of community branches are breaking
   of interlocking necessities are breaking
   what happens to breathing or seeing
      believing or being
      what happens what happens
      what happens what happens
   what happens what happens when
      what happens if

what happens here
at the end
/ after our deepest
forest.

* Poem written for the Pacure Nature Reserve Competition: Trinidad and Tobago

SHE WHO REMINDED ME WHAT MATTERS
for Tim Atkins

Waking with a whelp, a tiny prod
& head of fire
           of love
for you once more my rose bud
                   my dear girl
all quaver like when I try to change
all tears & limbs
       extinguishing the world
with one small tear or smile
– a wine drop in Seferis' sea –

    Let me not remember the trouble
of before you
       Besides, it was another country

    Let's look forward instead to blossom & ducks
walking – you precious bobble head – the way you fall
then a second's pause as you work out what feels
before caterwauling or a laugh – depending on what!
       Who knows the little mysteries of you, space worm
                           tiny stranger
come to save her mama
from not knowing what's important in life

    Here's to all the precious minutes
of every colour with each other & to papa
& to poems
       with happy endings.

TEN THOUSAND THINGS

The Reason that can be reasoned
is not the eternal Reason.
The name that can be named
is not the eternal Name.

The Unnamable is of heaven and earth the beginning.
The Namable becomes of the ten thousand things the mother.

Therefore it is said:
'He who desireless is found
The spiritual of the world will sound.
But he who by desire is bound
Sees the mere shell of things around.'

These two things are the same in source but different in name.
Their sameness is called a mystery.
Indeed, it is the mystery of mysteries.
Of all spirituality it is the door.

— From Lao Tzu, *The Tao Te Ching*,
trans. D. T. Suzuki and Paul Carus (1913)

SOURCES

Tao Te Ching, 'Lao Tzu'
Contributions to Philosophy, Martin Heidegger
Ten Thousand Things (the film), Jack Wake-Walker

The dog is a part of every human

experience. It is very happy on every one

of its limbs. It bites / does not bite

the hand that mocks it.

Besides which, leading a dog

to water means only one thing. River

's a mouth, the dog is endless. She cannot

change what she does not

see. Only

The stick is a thing to beat the human

with. The dog deserves this. Trailing

its tail in the dirt. Meanwhile we miss

beauty in all its small places. Have not

the patience nor courage to please the dog.

To not lead the dog. Intentionally.

What is the body for

if not this thing to beat us

with. But what is it for

now? Where is

our knowing when

it becomes nothing but

blind dust leading

the dust.

We have this thing. Isn't any

kind of complexity. Doesn't howl

when it's called. Human flowing

through dust. Basin of time.

Unsupportable howling. Man is

But what is woman therefore. In the scene

where he enters. And where,

the dog. Narration

that figures is closing. The net is it

tightening. When he will settle

/ forget. Her into the discourse.

When he will cut a line

into it, like a poem.

We have this thing

is it intentional.

Some think it is stick leading

dog. But is it the will leading

the moments, or beauty

leading the vice

versa can also work too. But of course

it does.

When you follow the time

is all backwards, is it all or apart.

When you follow this

had to add up to itself before

its presentment. And we who have time

at hand, as our stick, as our

eye leading the eye. Hand

held open to mock

What is that we are doing:

tradition, childhood, that wild

& whirring. That faux seeing.

Words are a net closing in

on the subject

of guilt, purpose, love

or presentment, swearing

blindness. Otherwise,

they are mirrors-for-

eyes. Either way dogs

do not have to bear all this

being four times more

grounded by earth &

sky.

But what is he doing now.

And what she is following

before him, leading him on

to the story of eyes.

It was older than that. It started

with she as matter

of course. No as he

as bones for eyes.

Taken as closing or doing

or wanting. Ha

he is – uh ah

– she has

started the game where

the dog is meaning

foregrounded, intent

is unknown.

No but how

known the dog is the she-wolf,

bitch is the earth. We come

after that meaning, suddenly

coming to life in this dangerous line

that does us no obvious good.

The thread is that too. But what were we

saying for. Dog is a dreamer who needs

to survive in the beauty's glow. Walking

that line is a line of much weight.

Many centuries flowing & pressing

on her but on him. And we dreamt

while we were awake.

Was this a terror of things. And we work

for that. Noiselessly toiling,

trailing our hopes in the dust

for the birds to follow our meaning

seed. Loam in our heart.

Sky is untouched, but the river

follows the bends of our meaning

obviously. Jumps ahead to the place

– we will be when we come

down to earth

for a final time. Before the beginning.

We have that terror, that hook

at the end of the line. Knowing always.

Dog does not have to bear so much

freedom or pain. Is mere cipher

of line, hook

for this story that's leading. Until

we start back at the end.

This might be a line about water. But what

if it's earth. What if all techne, all feeling

is buried in that. And we bury our line

in the river. Cannot but do that

each time. Knowing it

does us no good.

Now it is hatred of sleep. Now

laughter at watching the dog,

he debases himself. She is coming

over to life on that line

between terror &

lies. Lurking in flesh

or in water, in mother

or father. We dream merely

not to be replicas

of the earliest line. Total

reversals. And a feeling

comes over us

Of life for the second, no nth

time. In the beginning

man does her no good. But in the beginning

he offers us shelter & eyes. Yet

in the beginning the world is all beauty

while woman sleeps through this

wanting, desiring. Dog lurks

in the background frame. Cannot lead

its way out of this paradise. Needs lying.

Needs treating as equal

to dream or to techne, our masterful

doing of earth & sky.

The same is it background

these patterns, these clearings

of dust. The people that toiled

there in the desert, making

their way for our selves, but the water

is changing. Of flesh & of blood.

Line has caught up with itself

back on itself! Net has caught

nothing but eyes. A reversal

of fate, that dangerous fugitive line.

Does him no good coming over us

suddenly confident, suddenly

But we know this pattern

it comes from before. Leads

nowhere to dust. Know that

the sunset is tricking us into nostalgia

of good, or our dreaming is not

of our being. But ten thousand times

stronger than now

it's debased. Toiling.

Strange notion of good.

& our rhythms, our knowledge

is changing.

Our rhythms are a cause

for their ends which have crossed

the line. Our nets spread,

we have never felt so alive. Can't

believe it is wrong. Can't get over

not seeing our techne debase us,

our stick, beating the blind

that leads

nowhere but dust. Only

back to the start.

Arrogance of man –

that he contain woman

& world in a pattern like music,

disinterested meaning! The eyes

of flowers have more sense

to them, dog is more

real in its notions of who

feeds the hand it began with.

Rubbing that stick

but it won't, can't lead us

to water. Merely visions of

drowning, chimera

of life.

A feeling comes over us. Then

we reach back for its justification.

Or forward, presuming

so much. We presume to know

the end of this story

of line.

Where she goes

will be worth asking

where does she want

to go, with or without

following. The music

of flowers tells us more

than all our limitless imitations

of knowing. Our techne of dust,

It is ashes to loam. Will

fall in the water of all our

myth-making. Noiselessly.

But we have not

the patience to stop nor

to hear it.

Woman is sleeping. The dog

woke the bird &

her arrogant heart. Yet her body

is too worth watching. Might say

she has nothing to say

outside this line.

Might say that this light

which we all lead

is expensive & true,

when we ask ourselves

what is that true when we lose ourselves

to ourselves in the life

of mirrors of eyes. In the backwards

time. But there is

also this beauty!

Always this beauty

which pains us to bear

like the dog in the myth of the

line. This feeling which walks in

front, leads us. This mouth

which is hooked from behind.

And she loves, he loves

to be hooked for the dog that they

are in reverse. Everything's

Endless mirror. To what end

is we do not know. Following, leading,

lurking & dying. The worry

of eyes, euphoric death

of the self are just

so many patterns. Music

of mind.

This feeling has caused us

to smile for a time, for the dog

who played tricks on us, fed

from our mocking, is handled

with care till it loses

beauty. Then the mind is left

wondering

what happened to her, but what happened

to him.

There is a woman, a man there

has always been. Symbols of

woman, of man. Ciphers of

dog. When our lust tastes our eyes,

but when our childhood is deep

at the end of the line, at the start of

the place of its figuring,

there is

brutality. The expression

is love but we cannot lead that

to the drinking. Cannot lurk

after time.

We record these things only

after the fact. We are only

part element of this life. Or this time

we look passionately

(through tears) for some beauty

to save us this time

from our twisted & makeshift

stars. Forgotten the sky.

And we follow the dog star, the brightest

system we find, leading ourselves

by ourselves, follow unknowingly

visual death! So close to the earth

that we missed that completely.

But so strange that we almost

touched. Struck down

by memory of a moment

before our being, our

leaving the frame. With or without

the sensation of taste. With or without

companion of dust.

We look to our

line & compound

that upon dust, eye upon

eye. And the passion we once had

for our living gets wordless

& soulless, our movements,

our wonder, mirrored back

in the ten thousand moments

that make up a life – strange & alive.

Ten Thousand Things
By Emily Critchley

First published in this edition by Boiler House Press 2017
Part of UEA Publishing Project
All rights reserved
© Emily Critchley 2017

Design and typesetting by Emily Benton
emilybentonbookdesigner.co.uk
Typeset in Arnhem
Printed by Imprint Digital, UK
Distributed by NBN International

ISBN 978-1-911343-17-2